# BIG WORDS FOR LITTLE

Helen Mortimer & Cristina Tr

# Love

## OXFORD

UNIVERSITY PRESS

# Family

Love is at the heart of every family. Loving families come in all shapes and sizes.

# Hug

A hug is just one way that we can show our love.

Using kind and positive words can also say 'I love you'.

# Warm

It feels good to wrap up on chilly days.
And being loved makes us feel
warm inside.

Surrounding someone with love fills
them with strength and hope.

# Thoughtful

We can show our love by doing thoughtful things for someone or giving something up for them.

Love makes doing those things worthwhile.

# Special

If we know how important
and special we are, then
it helps us to love
and be loved.

# Loss

When we lose someone that we love,
we feel sad.

But we never have to say
goodbye to happy memories.

# Friends

Friends share fun and laughter but also problems and worries.

That is why we all need loving friendships.

**We're stuck!**

# Forever

Love doesn't run out or get used up.

It is always there for us to give to others and for others to give to us.

# Care

When we really care about someone we try hard to keep them safe and well.

Sometimes that means saying 'No'.

# No matter what

Love brings us close to each other.

It helps us to be kind, patient and open-hearted, no matter what.

# Home

A house is made with walls and a roof but a home is made with loving hearts and helping hands.

# Love

Love is such a special feeling.

All we need
is love!

# Ten ideas for getting the most from this book

**1** Take your time. Sharing a book gives you a precious chance to experience something together and provides so many things to talk about.

**2** This book is all about what it means to love and be loved. When was the last time you said, or heard, 'I love you'?

**3** It's also a book about language. Ask each other how you would put love into words.

**4** The illustrations in this book capture various moments at a farm park. We've intentionally not given the children names – so that you can choose your own and perhaps invent something about their personalities. What name would you give to their pet dog?

## Myrtle?
### Sniff?
#### Biscuit?
##### Dave?

**5** Sometimes we have used animals to express an idea: for example the concept that every family – however it is structured – is a loving unit.

**6** Each spread shows a snapshot of love in action. Why not talk about what might have happened before and after each moment that's captured in this book?

**7** Children can sometimes worry that there is a limited supply of love. We have tried to convey, using concrete examples, the unconditional and infinite nature of love.

**8** By exploring and recognizing the many different ways in which we express love and let it show in how we behave, we hope this book will give children and the adults in their lives the tools they need to make sense of their feelings and the world around them.

**9** Encourage imagination – what other animals would you like to meet in a farm park? Llamas, ostriches . . . dinosaurs? How would you show a T-rex that you loved her?

**10** You could each choose a favourite word about love from the book – it will probably be different each time you share the story!

# Glossary

**loss** – the sad feelings we have when someone
we love dies

**open-hearted** – if we are open-hearted, we feel
like being warm and friendly

**used up** – if something is used up, it is gone
and there is none left

**wrap up** – if we wrap
up, we put on
clothes to keep
us warm when
it is cold